W0115778

# blood
# mysteries

**Camino del Sol**

A Latina and Latino Literary Series

# blood
# mysteries

Dixie Salazar

The University of Arizona Press

Tucson

The University of Arizona Press
© 2003 Dixie Salazar
First Printing
All rights reserved

∞This book is printed on acid-free, archival-quality paper.
Manufactured in the United States of America

08 07 06 05 04 03  6 5 4 3 2 1

Library of Congress Cataloging-in-Publication Data

Salazar, Dixie.
Blood mysteries / Dixie Salazar.
p. cm. — (Camino del sol)
ISBN 0-8165-2237-5 (pbk.: alk. paper)
1. Women—Social conditions—Poetry. 2. Women prisoners—
Poetry. 3. Biculturalism—Poetry. 4. Women—Poetry. I. Title.
II. Series.

PS3569.A459187 B58 2003
811'.54—dc21

2002015441

British Library Cataloguing-in-Publication Data
A catalogue record for this book is available from the British
Library.

Publication of this book is made possible in part by the proceeds
of a permanent endowment created with the assistance of a
Challenge Grant from the National Endowment for the Humani-
ties, a federal agency.

# Contents

# Part 1 For Norma Jean and Others

## Amazing Grace

Oxidized bathing beauty
dives straight into the bubbled
asphalt of the Fresno Motel parking lot
swan dives through peroxide clouds
as if the Sands Motel
were still alive
with stubbed-cigar high rollers
Frederick's of Hollywood garter belts
and bloody Marys
stirred with grace
in the days when Esther Williams fell
sideways into synchronized stars,
the moon, a sequin pasted
on a satin sky.

Now Amazing Grace rolls
over the railroad tracks
from radios tuned to morning-after miracles.
But she's frozen vertical
through fermentations of diesel, Muscatel
and My Sin. She's there
for the working girls and the laid-
off strippers, for the busboy slit
open like a trout in 14C—
she's amazingly untagged and unmolested,
managed to keep her figure
though her maillot is edged in rust
and one topaz curl, burned white,
escapes from a tarnished bathing cap.

Still, she's got her form
though no Olympic-size pool awaits her,
no parallel lover soaked in baby oil
ready to peel her like an onion
her grace—amazing
considering all she's seen

and where she's headed—
straight down to the gutter
only seconds between her
and unforgiveness . . . or could it be
forgiveness? Aging siren
never growing older
diving for our sins—
for all the shipwrecked saints
and wretches among us.

# Nowhere Girl

*in memory of Sylvia, who took her own life, KVC\**

If you had found
a neck of woods
beyond the foothills
on the day when a mockingbird
was trying on the voice
of the rain,
becoming your idea
of rain
you might have seen a woman
the moths flew through
the spiders wove around
melting out of a landscape
spotted with shadows
washing her hands
in an empty basin of light
saying she didn't exist.

If you had touched the basin
a chill would cramp
your hand, a stone
turn to a grain of time.
And if you looked too hard
she'd evaporate
but her hands
would remain
to sign the words
of a song
that doubted all this,
and no matter
how hard you tried
to convince her before—
now, you'd open yourself

* Kingsview Psychiatric Center

to the question
to the transparent ticking
of the hands
with no clock.

# For Norma Jean

*(with apologies for the photograph my uncle took)*

Fractured scales fall
sadly into the Milky Way—
at the grand piano her painted fingers
roll open windows

release a cloud of wounded birds

where a stray dog snaps
a wing bone in two      their eyes meet
a soft explosion of feathers and heart
she gives him what he wants

greedy eyes fixed on her soul

stolen in small bits      hard
for her to say no
to the soft tug of mutual hunger
the terrible night vision of dreamless children

that she understood so well

that Bresson knew      breaking her fall
acrobat of F stops and sidelong glances
stealthy as a shutter speed
synced to her heartbeat
to the whisper of birthday candles

fat cigars and pacifiers
atomized clouds of My Sin
steam from a subway grate
all sold      like ponies at six cents a pound

brand new tears for a stranger

returned to a world of strangers

when Joe DiMaggio brought roses          and angels
doused themselves with green perfume
earthly essence of her last breath

equivocal voyeurs          even in death

her stars are cold with old desire
circle the lit mesas like vultures.
With popping flash bulbs          they sneak
into the morgue to snap her toes          they want

as usual          her body AND her soul

A black crow flies
through centuries of steeples and ruins
with a scrap of celluloid
a drop of silver          a blink of time
to weave a beautiful nest of tears.

# Celeste Pareé

Hunger scents the air
drifts in from miles of posted land
beyond Nuit Enchanté
and the mirror, ringed with naked
bulbs, her face disappears into.
Opening day of deer season—
the day is flushed
with new blood, cracks
with the hope of escape and surrender.

Her mother's signing
a cross in the clouds—
Father is cleaning his gun.
She's alone, practicing pliés
and acceptance speeches,
the soft flesh between
her toes, cut by fishnet
and secondhand toe shoes.
The mirror refracts her
beyond the paper swan
that churns in the air
with broken wings.

Tipped up to footlights,
his gray, expensive eyes,
her drowned blue ones
whisper, "Our Princess,
she's really going places."
Baby-salmon pink tints her cheeks
down to the sweetheart neckline
as she taps out
to "Lullaby of Broadway"
ready for the explosion
of faces, applause.
On a street disappearing
in fog, she stops to hook

an unlooped garter.
She's still young, and if
you asked where she was going,
she'd say, with no pause,
"Straight to the top."
It was never her plan
to be crowned
at the Chi Phi Sweetheart's Ball,
to sit on a red T-Bird
high heels pointed
for the benefit of the 20/30 Club
car wash, or to share the bill
again at the El Rey, with Domay
"Gorgeous Cherokee Half-Breed."

"Demure, darling and daring—
a special routine," it says
above two poufs of organza,
fishnet and shine.
Tobacco spit and cigar tips
gleam in burnt-sienna light.
Glass flares, throws from wall
to wall the push
of her belly against
their commingled heat,
the low rumble
of readiness, the in-
out of fermented desire,
the bruised aftermath
of hard light, struck
through a forest of faces,
all surrendering
to her, all after her
very softest spot.

# The Lost Underwear of Central Park

Pushing aside stiff
panties with his stick,
the old man stabbing
cans, moves closer
to the trembling wool coat,
gnawed bare in spots,
a patched dress hitched up
around her hips.

He watches her hand
in its private shiver
and the furious
rocking that lifts her
into the secret
palace of lost pleasures
beyond the bone-cold planks
of the thumping bench.

By the cinder path
he spikes a Stroh's.
In bruised flamingo light
he watches ducks unfold,
remembers a pair
of silk stockings once, caught
by the wind, a lake
where he saw their flight
how they arced and fluttered,
and the flaming hair, laced
with fragrance of jasmine and gin
how it whipped wildly—
a nameless animal
panting in his face, a perfumed
sting, and the dance
of her eyes, reflecting

the slipping away
of the day, wet green
going wet gray. Slowly, he turns
from darkening water, illusive
silk legs that loop
and tangle in his mind forever
kicking up and away.
The old lady smooths down
her dress, pieced with lonely
stains, large as the Hope diamond
steps over torn Fruit
of the Loom, where winter rye
is flattened under Midnight's
churning hips and seed pearls
scattered loose by tattooed hands
that couldn't wait.

# The Magic Hands Salon

*for Nellie*

For the first time in weeks
she changes from the peacock robe
bends to each of her nine kitties
and calls them by name
opens the slit of one blind
to the pale sky and the banners
of Save Mart she'll pass
on her trip to the Magic Hands Salon.

"Just between me and you honey,"
Ruth Ann dips forward
from the row of panting helmets,
"if Earl was to go tomorrow,
I wouldn't have me another one."
The air is thick
with the swarm of pastel lotions.
Ruth Ann hooks the pink robe

at her neck where a bead
of warm rinse slips down.
She allows her head to fall
backwards, balanced between
lavender fingers and fluorescence,
remembers giving herself
to that long ago cup of hands,
the baptismal water closing

over her face like sliding glass,
the distant stretch of hereafter,
the promise of palmettos,
letting go . . . the hymns washing
and rippling, voile dress
billowed up from her hips.

But instead of rapture,
the children's fat kazoo cries,

"Look at that lady's dress!"
and the fear of moccasins
chewing her feet.
Ruth Ann is combing her out
teasing the soft tiers.
"Oh honey, that's sweet."
In a cloud of swan's down hair
at her feet, she sees the face
of a man who survived
one hundred years of silence and ice.
She'll carry the polar cap blue
of those eyes with her when she shuts
the musical door, slides past
old Earl's lazy eye and "Faded Love"
from the Laundromat, lost
in her Siberian valentine,

one she never sent or received
that floats in the limbo
of memory like lost souls
sunken under miles of ice,
already melting into thoughts
of her kitties and sums
added in her head, figuring
if she cuts back on Home Shopping Club

and cough syrup, she can send
another fifty to the TV evangelist,
a plea for one more glass eye,
one more prosthetic device,
and for the same ebb and flow
of release, the seizure
that won't be denied, the laying
on of hands—all she's ever desired.

# Celebration Cake

*for Zelma Toney*

White bubble hairdo,
Wonder Bread skin
soft as oleo and eggs
she creamed together
with promises
of a paradise so sweet
you could serve it
on a paper doily
while lions and lambs
tangoed around fountains
of milk and honey.

If the Bible had not commanded
neighborly deeds and offerings,
her Oklahoma nature would have.
I accepted the cake and Watchtower
but questioned delayed
paradise, the family holding hands
knee-deep in heaven.
If I could give up Christmas,
birthdays, newspapers,
voting and questioning,
I could have life eternal.
That sounded fine
but I couldn't imagine
the eternal part,
the silver lining
without the cloud,
the party that never ended,
the parade of hot fudge sundaes
stretching to infinity—
fire without ice, found
without lost, answers
without questions.

Stabbed in her home,
no suspects, no signs
of breaking and entering,
the same bubble hairdo
but ten years older,
Zelma smiled sweetly
on the six o'clock news
while the voice-over
gave only the facts.
And so I re-ran the home movie
of her last hour
from my own imagining:
a shaggy man, high on paint fumes,
asking for a sandwich.
She wouldn't refuse,
wouldn't lock the door
or try not to witness,
offering Watchtower or scriptures
before the shadow fell.
And if she did plead
for her God's mercy,
she did not falter
in the silence that answered.

Through rooms of books
without a single answer
I pass into the kitchen
crack eggs in a bowl,
blend flour, sugar, buttermilk,
pinch of salt, nutmeg, questions
blend together, stir
a Celebration Cake to rise
upward, sweeten the rafters
to praise the lawns and alleys,
to praise the memory
of a neighbor's kindness,
to praise the known and unknown

because I want to believe
the unconditional love
of creation is simple
as the faded ink
on the rim of a recipe card,
the single word, "Delicious!"
a word that praises the cake
and taste bud both, syllables
that celebrate the sweet
flow of saliva
and the floating wafer, the bond
of belief and question.

# Crazy Quilt

*Materials were assembled that were never born for each other;
its plan of construction suggested the splintered points left by a
stone in its passage through a window; pattern it cannot be
called, for pattern is ordered relation.—Susan Johnston,* Early
American Patchwork Quilt Designs

**Remembrance**
Counting under her breath
      she pieces a crazy quilt
setting the blocks—
      boxcars, the sun clicks between
                Cat's Paw
           laid over the Windowpane
Grady's mustache scalloped
         with chicken fat
      grease maps on the magazine
Chevron sky
     Cookie Cutter stars and moon
         scraps of the lost BOOK OF DAYS.
Skeins of wool fuzz window lights
           easy to slip
      into cocoons of floss and dropped
        stitches, sleepwaltz
           to memory's fiddle beat
      eyes patched with velvet
        railroad ties.


**Crown of Thorns**
    Nannie Sue gets up
      off the floor—
        still feeling the hook
   of his cane in her waist
           wrist on fire, fingers find
        the chipped ivory
         pick up the hymn

where she left off
　　　　　window where the sun drops
splattered with tobacco juice,
　　　　　pain, a darning needle
he poked in Jesus' eye.
　　　　　She decides to ignore
the measured stamp
of a rubber-tipped cane
　　　　　　　　Old Grandad stenciling
the settee arm—keeps her eyes
　　　　　　　　on a dripping heart
a tintype smile
framed with Nell's long, blonde braid.


**Sister's Choice**
　　　　San Francisco's fog burns off
　　　　　　by noon.
Above, the freeway shudders—
　　　　　　joists dance around her
　　　　　　　　hairline cracks like Featherstitch—
　　　below, the fault line waits
　　　　　　for a signal from the moon.
　　A stinging in her eye remembers
　　　　　　the smoke shed
　　　　　　where Daddy cured hams . . .
the present rings her back
　　　　　　to Sister on the phone
　　　quoting Revelation, Chapter seventeen
　　　　　　　verse five.
She holds firm, anchors herself
　　　　　　in Honeycomb wings
　　　Dog's Ears lace
　　　and ribbons
　　　　　　　　twisted into Sunday School braids
　　　third prize chess pie
she holds onto the quilting hoop
　　　　　　as if for her life

19

sky crackles above
earth crackles below
she rides the swells
eyes closed, holds on
and crawls into tufted dreams
replicas of the seven-year-old's
safe beneath Storm at Sea.

## Wheel of Fortune

Wheel of Time flashing
back to jitterbug toes
a Duck's Foot in the Mud

a shadow-stitched fan.
Nell's smoke satin dress
shimmied with Diamond Stitch
and dog tags snapped at carnival neon
a chicken scratched for a dime
wash of colors
trimmed in Fishbone stitch
ferris wheel diving
Lazy Daisy Long-tailed whine
swatches of color flashed
over the silver feed dog
of the Singer treadle.
Whatever became of the lard tin
she carried her daddy's dinner in
to the sorghum mill?
All-night fire
vigil of stoking, a long cigar
night air, thick, soaked with stars
gummy and sweet
brown juice ran down
Ladder Stitch along the bottom
best Sorghum in Spring Hollow.

**Variations**

Death squeals bleed
through her dreams
red morning sky
a Sunburst Variation
anniversary roses burst open—red
on the Catch Me If You Can
she uses for a tablecloth.
But they're butchering hogs
in the yard again
her sister hides
under Pinwheel blades
carpet slippers over her ears
harping to herself the same verse.

**Soldier's Return**

She picked up the snapshot
of him at his desk
saw the photo in the photo
of the woman smiling
just like he'd said in letters
from the front
where he took dictation
and filed death certificates.
He wrote to her picture he'd said
but it wasn't her
in the picture on his desk.
She knew that hat
a Feathered Star and the ring
a variation of her own
from wedding pictures
of his first wife.
She bent over the loom
rings interlocked within rings
plunged the needle in
and out—she won't forget
Double Wedding Ring
for his bed
in his room.

21

**Illusion**

Foggy patches drift
and disappear.
She sees herself in the picture
window, like a memory patched
between fiction and truth, sorrow and joy.
Soon she'll sleep
under plaid pansies
stitched together
from soft, old shirts
wide ties, juice-stained aprons,
her lost sister's pinafores.
Each block picks up
another thread, adding
its trace of paisley, stars,
acorns, dots, cornflowers
and tiny lighthouses
sewn into wings or wheels
that tell the whole story
a nest
stitched with ticking
a haven
where she can exist
between remember and forget
pieced together
maybe not the truth
but a Crazy Quilt
lapped with color and smell
kitchens and Sunday afternoons
parasols, Blue Waltz perfume
windmills embroidered with names
she no longer knows
because they fray in the wind
like silk raveling along the railroad tracks.


**Mosaic**

Wiping drool from his lapel
she cleans the soup from his mouth
sponges his arms

22

lets down his bed—
This is her time now
when her half sister        the moon
is worked with an Overcast stitch.
Lips sewn into a tight seam
she punches the needle
into a clock-sized circle of silk
bone thimble slips
as she rises
opening doors, crooked on hinges
where frames don't meet
searching for her glasses
through rooms of fog
and Tennessee Lace
rooms where the colors meet
in a blurred Mosaic
memories of the sunset
through broken windows.

# Valley of Shadows

In the valley
of lengthening shadows
spores whirl in the wind
grass pickerel nudge
into muddy clouds.
I'm here on a dare
no one remembers

but me, and now the path
is blocked by a fallen log
with lover's names buried
in wood, and rings
within rings, exposed
by the felling.
A line of ants shows me

it's a bridge
and I balance myself
on their homes
tunneled into the wood.
Determined to cross
I plough forward
though the wood is soft

and there are no markers
or maps, and my guidebooks
are filled with useless marks
old cipherings
and words from a foreign
tongue, stolen from my mouth
and never returned.

I decide my tears
are moonstones made
by the daily grind

of the tides, salt falling
through an hourglass,
that trees darken hard
as diamonds just because

God says so,
and that tugging at my skirt
is something large with wings
or my soul throwing shadows
on the wall scratched with names
from two worlds, twin moons
risen from a new translation.

# Part 2 Still Life with Cactus and Magnolia

# Taking It Back

Hand tinted, creamy olive skin,
green eyes, ripe and innocent
clear as the holy water
she dipped into at High Mass,
Bella, my Spanish grandma
smiled shyly across the hall

at Grandma Winnie, pale
as bleached muslin, as white-
washed Southern porches built
by French and English Protestants,
though her eyes sparked
like Indian flint dug up from red soil.

Like fugitives or outlaws on the lam,
we moved away, changed
the spelling of our last name,
the one on the ID bracelet
flushed down the toilet,
never taken off before—

the one that had studded my suitcase.
With my brother's pen knife
I pried off the letters
slowly, with great effort
and left white, reverse scars
where the Spanish name had been.

"What is she?" his mother asked,
perplexed, I could tell
by neutral skin tone and hybrid name.
"She's a mutt," he laughed, ruffling
my hair backward as if waiting
for me to lick his hand.

Marriage could solve this, I thought,
this dilemma of spellings
and explanations that spelled
out shame. But taking his name
meant more than just giving mine
away—that part was easy—

when the fingertip veil fell
a white curtain hanging
between layers of history,
I signed the new name easily,
the crisp one syllable,
so Germanic, so acceptable.

On the inside covers
of the Little Golden Books
I find in a trunk, on each
there is a dark, scumbled spot
where the old spelling is gouged out,
leaving a white, open wound.

After reading through choices
I always check "other"
not Chinese, Eskimo, White,
or Hispanic because nothing
fits. But "other" also fits
nothing.

In a black, marble room
lit by one bare, overhead bulb
in slow dancing dream time,
I float from slab to slab—
lift the white sheets and shake
my head, leaving each body
(though familiar) unidentified.

It is the same girl who dressed
in musty, moth-bitten mink

and clomping high heels, also known as
Dolores or Della Street,
who looks back at me,
laminated for the DMV, spelled

backward through time,
like a ghost girl passing
through different bodies to come here
to take back what never
belonged to anyone, what
still splits off in the wind.

# Still Life with Cactus and Magnolia

Let's say there's a hat
still warm in the crown
from Mass, mother-
of-pearl hat pin swallowed
in a foamy veil, long,
dark quill of pheasant
feather intersecting
the raggedy cactus
cold light dribbles over.
Let's say we find a dish
of pesos and dimes
wound with a hand-tooled belt
and speckled trout winds
seeping under the sill
where suede high heels
returned, soaked with night.
Cigar ashes sift
into the inclement face
of open pocket watch.
Now replace the belt
with a beech wood rosary
rubbed smooth to thwart
the belt's growing suppleness.
Let's say your own life
hangs in opposing drafts
of wind from chinaberry
to piñon limbs—then kisses
might never be blown
to a disappearing train.
As the pearl-green Sheaffer's ink
fans over magnolia appliqués,
maps of Memphis and a rosary
coiled to strike letters
marked Department of War,
who's to say what will twine
with what, and which paths

will intersect as stars collide
from the four stations
of the heart.
And the girl who has rubbed
her Gypsy Rose Red lips
will kiss her papa's forehead
as if still fresh with prayers
from evening Mass, as if
she had not already crossed
the threshold, uncrossing
herself forever.

# American Meltdown

Angel's in love with this white
girl who props her Nikes
on the Rush bumper sticker
of her father's Volvo.
She taunts him with
the pale swish of her ponytail
and her washed-out eyes.
Angel reaches for her
through twilight fire
and the diamonds
of her father's chain link.
At night, an albino moon
drives him mad
with blonde circulations.
Giving in to an old gravitational
pull, he knots his body
into white bedsheets.
It's nothing new—
the easy attraction
of pendulum points
the absence of light
seeking light, the desire
to conquer the conqueror.

He wakes in the cold
bath of his own heat,
ducks, then accepts
the blows she rains
on his head, throws
his history book to the wind,
lets the simple juice
of spring fill him
like every stem and vein
in gold confusion.

Watering hydrangeas
after dinner, I watch their dance
of fire, the sky filled
with the sparks of their contact.
I think of my father
who buys American cars,
married Anglo like his brother,
and now his great-grandchildren
are only one-eighth of him,
no one speaks Spanish
and the meltdown is complete.

In a dizzy whoop of love
and pain, Angel calls to her.
Their arms tangle dark
and light. Half of me
wants him to stop, pull
back into the safety of shadows,
and half of me wants
him to lose himself
in the heart's crucible,
to melt with her
and reach the fusing point
of a new element.

## Angel of Brown Street

Sweet Angel has grown
too cool to play street games
trading insults with his brother's
friends, from the sidelines
under a Raider's cap.

I give them flat tennis balls
they pop up to a thumbprint moon,
throwing beautiful Aztec curves
their new muscles trace
burnt arms offering

all they have to the sky
to the narrowing light
of dinner's onion breath
climbing upward to chase
itself in circles, to blend

with fumes and filaments,
chorizo and tired prayers,
the half cries of Angel
cracking the dark tomb
of his manhood open.

He spits in the street
like a man, flirts wildly
with passing cars
that miss him by inches.
"Hey, puta homeboy

can't even catch a cold."
Their ball has landed on a roof
with Rudolph, hanging three months
now since Christmas
by a rope tied to a deflated hoof

limp angel flown too close
to the sun, where paramedics
once hauled down the man,
strapped on a gurney,
gone mad, calling P.G.&E.

to stop pumping gas
down his chimney,
to give him back his striped cat
they tried to poison
while the neighborhood watched.

Now Angel is on the roof
with heavy wings,
dropping burnt-out lightbulbs
instead of tennis balls
down onto their open mouths.
But the Armenian grandson's ghost
appears, the failed salesman
of Christmas, and Tom
with his alcoholic Rudolph nose
and paper cup of beer,

Mrs. Knight in her wheelchair,
all the evicted ghosts
of Brown Street, offering advice—
"stay in school," says Mrs. Knight,
"do your best and you'll succeed."

Tom tips his cup as if to drain
the blushing rosé sky,
but none of this
not even his homeboy's desertion
will bring him down.

Already he's failed at stealing
bikes, and no good

at gang banging
he shunts from one
continuation school to another,

unlike Gilbert, his brother
whom everyone loves—
his father's look-alike
who only has to wink
or spread his wings and smile.

So we leave him there
cool Angel, hunched in fog,
Christmas lights
and collapsing reindeer
waiting for the first updraft
or for one good reason
to descend, trapped
between the gap
of borrowed earth
and impossible heaven.

# At the Ponce de León Apartments

The sun buzzes and slides
under bloated eucalyptus leaves
and a chemical blue perfume.
Cheetos, tamale husks, Rainbow crumbs,
Barbie's high heel, a Monopoly hotel
and Lotería cards, the sun and boot
spilled onto sticky cool deck.

Face down on a chaise, Mary Estrella
dozes in a cocoon of sunspots and cocaine
from a pink shell beside her bed
dreaming of abuela's long gray braid
tethered to her belly button, just above
the crescent liposuction scar—
dreaming of unmarked graves and spending
foreign currency. Her dreams splash up
from some lost cousin dreamer
looking for fountains, finding
flamingos and fever instead—
but what good is it to carry
genes from one column to the next?

But if, for one moment, she could shut out
the crisscross of jet engines,
leaf blowers breaking the sound barrier,
and snowstorms choking her head
she might hear a voice calling
her lost name, long ll's dragged
behind the boat with her profile
at the helm, a weathered figurehead
with folded wings and splintered lips
the wind sighs through, searching
for an open mouth to receive
its host, to give the right response
the one her lips were molded for.

# Piñon Nuts

We begged him to teach us Spanish
but he wouldn't. Here in the heart
of America, skin tones
and tongues were homogenous
as milk from purebred cows.

We heard Spanish once a year
in Colorado where Grandpa
sold used cars at the Rainbow garage
after the Depression wiped out
a city block of his stores

and left him bitter as the juice
of venison strips he gnawed,
escaping into his camper
with its false bottom for hiding deer
shot out of season.

Ignoring postal regulations,
he mailed us deer meat, bleeding
in a bed of piñon nuts,
telling Bella, "¿Que tiene Ud.?"
then, "Shut up" in English.

Bella went off to Mass
in their newest Chevy
and a velvet dish hat
chosen from over a hundred,
one for every fight they had.

His father died with the sheep
in a blizzard, Grandpa saved
by stuffing his feet in a foxhole.
His namesake, my father, got whipped
every time Grandpa saw him.

'59, snowdrifts high as frozen waves,
forced to turn back two miles past
timberline, they found Grandpa's name
and date of the day before carved
on a tree, his last deer at seventy-three.

After Bella died, he slept
on the broken spine of the back porch,
wouldn't eat or take his insulin,
telling her photograph or anyone
who'd listen, how much he loved her.

Each letter began, "Corazón
de mi corazón," a courtship
in a graveyard, words poured out
again later for her picture.
In between were all those hats.

Rainbow trout swimming in fat,
empanadas, flaky and sweet, a bowl
of piñon nuts, Grandma making faces
behind his back. "Montaña, huevos, sal,"
bits of Spanish she taught us . . .

and a swish of hats on a wall—
all that's left. In Spanish class
today, I learned "piñon" meant pine
and rolled the word in my Anglo mouth
like a sweet, round nut.

# I Always Check "Other"

Other can be a place,
a residence for those of us without
papers, where halos of lightning bugs
swarm the rickety family tree

where tails of comets glow
like radioactive black-eyed peas
and Virgin Mary nightlights
burning a hole in the soul's valentine,

the laboratory of the heart
where the alchemist's daughter
never sleeps, blending opposites
re-inventing the kingdom of self

or the dream of a lighthouse beam
sweeping through magnetic storms
of self-doubt, the checkmark pointing
like a needle to not exactly true . . . north.

# Rewriting History

No one remembers
who discovered this or that
river, or the hypotenuse
of rain, blurring a name
etched in window breath
snatched from your mouth
as you pledged allegiance to shame

or none of the above history—
Davy Crockett grinning down bears
but not mispronunciations of his name—
*that* you could understand, but not
the reason for spelling it wrong, knowing
it was wrong . . . a deliberate change
of facts, unmemorized in mutinous clouds of chalk.

An angel was sighted, skimming
the chalkboard, writing down names
for detention—fingering the guilty
and innocent who merged in white starch
and pleats, tight as little fists
of true and false—answers united
for one nation, invisible to all.

And then the terrible bell called you
to dodge ball and hard asphalt
you had to bob and weave, to hide
in the open . . . a secret exposed . . . to dance
on a dime when your name was called—
you had to choose sides . . . and nothing
you'd ever memorized was on the test.

Part 3 Night Life

## Virtual Reality

Then
I wore paisley,
bought Wayne Newton records.
That was where the bus left me,
stunned by whitewashed stucco,
dim memories from a strange address,
the known face's unfamiliar name.
Then I shrugged,
said it didn't matter
tried to match myself
to the irregular heartbeat,
to the cold furrows
dug into an unmade bed,
took up archery and needlepoint,
swallowed slivers of glass
and smiled at cocktail parties
into mirrors, trapped
in the infinity effect.

Later
I denied it all,
Wayne Newton,
buying the maple dinette,
the hands that knew my darkness
inside, the way I opened
to them, the odd way
the man lay, contented
and contorted both,
the way the stars staggered
in a trance, whispering
the death wish of my sister
the moon, where a road burned
into the night
calling me to dark windows
reflecting back the open doors.

Now
I am here,
but there still exists,
and that slight flutter of the curtain
could only be frayed breath
come back from a great distance
a reminder of who I am,
and that flash up my spine
the last shudder of a falling
star, the breath of a wish
to be someone else.
And that humming that comes after,
the alternating current
of then and now,
and somewhere between,
the truth, that has nothing to do
with any of this.

# Rain at Night

falls through
the fiddleneck ferns
soft jazz for the romance
of Rainbows and German Browns.
Slowly, the rivers rise,
swollen with the taste
of soap, perfume,
acid, glue, sweet and sour,
the ink bled
from notarized documents,
nurse's charts, valentines,
milk of venom
rich as the lining
of a womb,
Lavoris, antifreeze
and happy hour margaritas.
Slowly, watery shadows
rise, the room spattered
with light, the smell
of wet leaves
the tapping of raindrops
on the tin roof
of dreams. We wake
with the taste of rain
salty on our tongues, a song
for the darkest crevice
of our souls
that only the light
of morning can drown.

# Why I'm Not Someone Else

This is an old story.
If my mother hadn't let
that soldier buy her a Scarlett O'Hara
in the Sweet Gum Lounge,
and if those two nervous molecules
hadn't bumped together
in the great cosmic elevator
neither you nor I
would be reading this now.

If your grandfather had been
an archeologist, mad about Homer,
he might have christened you
Agamemnon, by laying
a copy of the Iliad
on your head, instead
of the cranky feed salesman
who married the muscular gym teacher
and called you Northrup instead.

And if my grandmother's
first suitor hadn't been struck
by lightning, and she hadn't fallen
for the used car salesman
who courted her in the cemetery
then I might have been
the famous Australian soprano
a shy French chef named his peach dessert
after, or the identical twin

who almost killed you, boring
a dart smack in the center
of your back when you were ten.
And if the gypsy who turned

your palm upward
to the Mona Lisa sky had seen
that slice of moon hooked over
the eaves like a secret smile,
she never would have dared predict

your mother's amazing luck,
the conversation overheard by the nurse
on the bus, and our story wouldn't be
our story, and we might be
like Cary Grant and Deborah Kerr,
passing in separate taxis
missing train connections because of a goat
you going up in the elevator,
while I'm going down.

# Klezmer Music

When the blonde gypsy
with the Mary Kay Cadillac
read between the lines
of her palm,
the summer bride sealed
her tears in wax,
lifted the veil
and tossed her garter
to the blue-eyed goat.
She kicked up
her raggedy train
and danced on the tiny taboret,
red- and white-striped stockings
twirling like barber's poles.
The sound of wounded peacocks
flew out of her throat,
a cat on the back porch,
locked in heat
or bedsprings of reunited lovers.
Her noisy heart
couldn't keep up
with fiddlestick feet
or the rattle of crepe
in the wind, but nothing . . .
not gossip, not lumbago,
or the sight of all that black,
not even klutzy Uncle Fiezel
with his steel-toed boots
could keep her down,
not with her fingertips
and toes on fire,
not with her heart slamming
like a screen door left ajar
in the wind,
not with all her cells given over
to the wild sounds that spun
her and the dizzy moon.

# Home Alone—Saturday Night

Baby moons ride low,
rake into cherried maroon,
hair, teased to the stars.

I want to be that flip
of chiffon, furled
in red convertible fumes,

spilling Wild Turkey and songs
across wet fields, light
slipping by on a neon wing.

Instead, wishing for the moon,
I'm watching it dance
in the Tiger Gar's trail

while Houdini hangs upside down
on my old black and white.
Slowly, the bubbles rise . . .

the pendulum wags,
my hands, folded like linen napkins
wait in the exhilaration of fishes

and tiny, gasping mouths.
Distant and immobile, I watch—
all the while, effervescent inside.

Hearing faraway jazz
and zodiac thunder, I sip a beer
grow warm and sleepy.

Later, wrapped in velour,
a train calls to me—
the perfect mesh

of sadness and longing.
I want to get it just right
because I'll need it later

and because everyone who rides
a slow train or fast convertible
comes to the same place,

but perhaps, like Houdini
locked and sunk in a voluntary tank
it is possible to escape,

leaving nothing but a drop of ink
a perfect description of a train vanishing
into the new moon's black disc.

# "Crazy Little Thing . . ."

*"People do not know how dangerous love songs can be."*
*—James Joyce*

When his cousin twitched her hips,
ran pink lips over virgin
ice cream in time to piano
licks of "Great Balls of Fire"
Jerry found out how dangerous
that sweet verb could be. Better used
as a noun, solid
as the rear axle of Elvis' gold limo
where he rocked alone,
whispering "love me tender"
into the capsule of smoky glass—
the same notes rising
and falling, condensed
on the back windshield
of a classic Chevy, warm breath meeting
cold glass, drawing a thin membrane
between the stars. She gasped,
a quick, orgasmic torch
like a breath of fire, or the flip
of a Zippo in the wax museum
where the hunk of love burned
under a cool glaze of wax,
and unchained notes smoldered
live as embers in the Graceland grate
blue-hot as magma layered with ice.

Two lovers kiss
in the shivery walk-in
of Apetito Fuerte, neon
blinking, "Caliente y Rapido."
He's melting in her ruffled arms
dissolving like a pelvis bone
in the boreal Memphis ground

where the feverish caretaker
prunes the King's roses. Coughing
up blood, he sucks his cigarette,
a cold, red rose lit against the night.
He whistles the broken melody
of Piaf's gypsy who steals and kills
for love, follows his lover
into the bowels of earth, the tunnel
of love, filling like an aorta.

At ten, smoking in the mouth
of the abandoned fire escape,
we divided love into two spheres,
the kind you like and the kind you marry.
Those who are lucky get both, balance
on the brink of a cold "ring
of fire," ready to fall
or dive in head first, despite
every song rising from the flames.

# Saturday Night at Albertsons

*(with homage to Ginsberg)*

Somewhere between
the Bosc pears, bologna
and Bruce Lee videos,
voices of hungover angels
wing down from the two-way
clouds above, sing na-na-na
live for today
and don't worry 'bout tomorrow . . .
but no one hears
pinching avocados and dipping
into the cashew bins,
price-comparing canned peaches
and adult diapers,
fondling Martha Stewart's
"Cold Weather Tips"
and headlines announcing
that Allen Ginsberg has died
na-na-na-na
live for today
"Does Your Boyfriend Lust
After Your Underwear?"
"Is the Earth Running
Out of Penumbras?"
No one seems worried . . .

everyone trusts
in the plastic cornucopia
overflowing with neon fruit
in the silo
of sugar and saturated fats
where someone's mother
hides glazed doughnuts inside her coat,
where the old man
in fez and bedroom slippers

kneels down in frozen foods
praying to an eggbeater,
where a draft of cold air circulates
like water round a drain,
as the sliding doors swish-swish
drowning, then rescuing screams
of the eternal crying baby on aisle six,
as the rented cop loafs and dares
his soul, spits twice
in the parking lot
slippery with the full moon's light.
na-na-na-na
live for today
Can we handle any more perfection
than this?

# Meteor Showers, Yosemite

If, when a blind moth
eclipses the moon
outside of time
you can't see wishes
re-lit from the tail
ends of old wishes—
look up from a bed
of eyeless needles
to the owl's cry
vaporized into a streak
of light, a spark
stirred from the hot
bed of smoky stars,
little deaths you must
be ready for
with all your eyes.

# Part 4 Casualties

# Our Lady of Trash Day

From a pile of amputated
peach limbs, headless Barbies,
an orphan flywheel,
a third-place science fair ribbon,
one string of burned-out Christmas lights
and a scorched, glittery wing
she kneeled in one-handed prayer—

the other snapped off—
a feeble call for time-out
become a plea for mercy
for pity on the burned-out heart.
But someone had painted one eyebrow
higher and smeared the left eye
to a sad, yet manic stare—

postpartum depression
or the bruised wink of a strung-out suppli-
cant
smelling of vodka and Vicks VapoRub
or dark circle of weariness
to match the twin that jabs her back
like a needle stitching her sweat
into the seams of Gap sweatshirts?

But even as succulents collapsed
and citrus exploded from inside,
I rescued her from a bed
of black ice, the certain crushing
of frostbitten jaws,
an eternal commingling
with moldy diapers and used razor blades.

Tired, overworked statue—
plaster receptacle of petitions
and foolish pleas: take away gout

and carpet stains, give me give me
silicon cleavage, diamond chia pets
and tattooed eyebrows.
She's been waiting a long time

to give up her tiny, painted heart
crammed full of secondhand guilt
and incomplete miracles
to be delivered into another life
reborn to convalesce in a new
reverence for ordinary morning light
and the sound of a one-handed rosary.

# Contact Visit

*"To place one's finger on a human body is to touch heaven."*
—*Novalis*

They come into the room crying,
Mercedes and three of her seven children
the front of her green jumpsuit wet,
her face swamped with tears.
For this hour of contact
they can't let go, full
of the feel and smell of each other
gummy bears, child sweat
milk-sweet hair and night wind.
For now it all drops away—
how she sold their Nintendo for a dime bag
how she was fed habañeros at five
for a joke, the beer her padre gave
to wash it away, how he knocked her
spilling milk, put her down
on the floor to lick it up,
then chipping at fourteen, falling in love
with heroin, the horse that rides her now.

For now it all drops away
Kotex Christmas tree the C.O.s revoked
beeping gates and doors that slam
like car crashes, skinny windows in tiers
where even the sky is locked out.
LaKeisha watches him watch her
a stranger whose brown eyes
are soft as melting chocolate—
the other two are lost
in the system, but now he pulls
her nose, an unfamiliar knob.
For the longest, she couldn't see him
when she closed her eyes.

65

Now his legs splay open
like a broken nutcracker, won't close—
that's the crack, she says, holding him
like a sack of flour
she may not be able to afford.

Later when they're told to strip,
bend over and cough, the muddy dark
will leak back a lost child cry
trapped in the walls like a wounded prayer
a bird roosting in dark rafters
between memories of wind
and cold cement.

But for one hour it all drops away and leaves
the touch of all flesh that brings them here
salacious, felonious, holy
holding them together inside
a broken shard of time, one hour
all the power and glory
of earthly touch they can hold.

# Casualties

Yellow tulips streak
in the wind where band practice
booms softly on the horizon.
A news update cuts into Mozart
carried down from the kitchen
window on the wind.
Digging, nails fill with a darkness
that wants to resurrect
anything at all.
But ruthlessly, I must clip back
the dead, pulpy bodies
of succulents that lift up
into my palm like limp toupees.
Banners fly from antennas
and schoolyard fences
a fever of kicking butt fills the air.

Last week's list of casualties
that slid into a bed
of rotting begonias
unfolds under my trowel.
Strings of ants stream
over soggy headlines and eye sockets
of a bird carcass, a cup
open to the rain.
Crumpled faces follow me
where I sprinkle snail bait
over violets, flatten
crisp shells they've left behind
like abandoned army tanks.

Turning over compost,
blackened leaves and orange peels
unlace and fall, sow bugs
and beetles stir wet leaves,
carrot and apple parings

into a thick soup of humus.
There is nothing to do
but clear away the frostbitten
bodies, count the losses
counting backward against the wind
and the anthems still chilling
the air like frost.

# Drawing Lesson / Negative Space

*for Michele at CCWF\**

The yard is down
when she scratches
by moonlight on tag board
stolen from commissary trash—
her eyes like the moment
between a match's scrape
and flare, oblivious
to the night sergeant's light
flaring over spikes
and razor points.

She doesn't see
a white bird against the dark
instead, a bird-shaped
cutout of sky
and rolls of barbed wire,
loopholes for angels
to slip into her new
second sight, to dance
on the cusp
of a nonexistent moon.

Sulfurous light adjusts
to her eyes that see Van Gogh
in skinny strips of stars
that used to be windows.
Roomie stealing tampons
third day of lockdown
no longer matter—
nor the key
as the space she draws
around it takes shape.

* Central California Women's Facility at Chowchilla

## Blong in America

Wake up Blong
You are in America
and the shoes you walk on
instead of in, were made for pavement
so cold your feet could stick
your breath become a bell
of white vapor, the slippery
English vowels spilling out
to follow you down the street.

I shake him awake again.
At his desk he kicks off
his bent shoes, draws pretty girls
and rows of hearts in margins
of conjugated verbs.
On a string around his neck
hangs a plastic heart with pink
plastic stones and hermetically sealed
LOVE, an amulet, he says, to chase
evil spirits like the one
that circled his house all night
a red-eyed, smoky cat
he wants to catch
and cook for lunch.

A disc of sunlight
burns over his shoulder,
skims the Mekong in search
of a resting place. Canary clouds
shatter its dance, streaking
the sky yellow as egg yolks.
He reaches into a pocket
of flitting fish and lifts
one by its oily fin. The river ferries
his coarse laugh back

from the farthest shore, an echo
in the haze of dusk.
When the new moon answers,
the river will open its arms
and receive the bodies
of drowned children
tied to each other with rope, linked
to a world of promises, better
only than their fears.
When one goes down, they all
go, but the boy who drags them across
swims on, won't know
till he reaches the other side.

Wake up Blong
You are in America
and we have read the story
of the first Thanksgiving
how the white man and red sat down
to a feast of gratefulness
of strange roots and shared seeds
in a new world, an American fairy tale
we want you to believe.
"Eggs, cookies, candy, lettice *(sic.)*, peach—
my breakfast," he says. "Milk, meat,
fish, birds, ham, pig, fox, crab" for lunch.
"Dinner is pork, fish, pig, gote *(sic.)*, hot dog."
For the assignment, he lists them
like I asked, misspelled samplings
from the menus of two worlds.

Concerned about the sleeping,
I ask if he was injured in the war.
He shows a long, forked scar
that meanders over his ribcage
like a red river marked on a map,
mumbles about an operation

in his hoarse, half-muted voice.
"What was it for?" I ask.
He shakes his head, "Almost I die."
He laughs, shuffling bare feet.
"My wife grows a baby. She's fourteen.
The Welfare asked her questions
like did she want to marry me?"
Again he laughs
like he's made a great joke.

With a stick he draws
lopsided hearts in the dust,
sweet onions wilting nearby
with ginger root.
"Blong . . . Blong . . ." the wind calls—
Grandma's fire far
from his thoughts, as the words
stroke his cheek like lips
of a girl he knows,
imagines they float and skid on the wind.
A silver ball spins toward him
from her shiny, open arms.

Wake up Blong
You are in America
and again you have missed the story—
a man who slept
for a hundred years, who woke
in a new century, a man like you
risen to a world moved on
without him.
Eyes sticky and full of sleep,
he is wearing a Pro-Choice t-shirt
and I ask him if he knows what it means.
He rasps his laugh, shrugs
and slides past me to the lunch truck
where he buys a Mountain Dew

to sip with sticky rice scooped
from tin foil with his hands.

Bees swarm the poppy's sleep
the day buzzes and hums
the sun already heating up
morning's griddle.
Into blue mist, a strip of smoke unfurls.
Wake up Blong,
your wife has made your favorite
boiled goat and fried baloney,
your son floats
through centuries of lapping,
warm in a sea where he flips
like a fish eager to swim,
to reach the distant shore,
to stretch upward to flickers
of warm light, where music beckons
where known and unknown pulses
call him, where everything is promised.

# Cricket at CCWF*

Can you hear it
trilling between
Kotex boxes
and blue toilet water
in a cold, cement corner?
A song, dragged up
from the bed of a river
or a tin cup of rain,
song of old shine,
luck and hard time
born of a sweet
and dirty friction—
pebbles, grains of salt,
ashes, mice droppings,
cake, spit and random dots
rubbed between wings
of innocence.
Bend down now
and lift it
into a paper cup,
a wet song tossed
back to the wind,
a curse, a prayer,
a tiny voice
croaking out one last
reprieve for us all.

* Central California Women's Facility at Chowchilla

# Doing the Dishes

Wide blue aviaries sleep
in memories with water
that pings in a pan
like bells in the mist
from the monastery—
every ping, the tick
of past and present
devotions, every ping
another name on a wall
of names for the birds
to bless.

Mockingbird songs
pour through greasy windows,
a warning to something
dark that stalks the sun.
Dreaming, I lift palms
filled with small windows,
reflections of fires
burning across centuries,
and the face of a woman
caught in the crossfire
of everyday light
and foreign investment
floating too close to a flame
that now flares up
from even the filthy skin
of used dishwater.

Dishes, rinsed and stacked
soapy water slips
through fingers with memories
of their own—they sign
to the new moon, black and sticky
despite soap and other miracles.
A.M. radio crackles

peace talk and smart bombs.
Perched on the sill,
as if to flit away,
the light is cool
and oriental, all that remains
between the flash
of that world and this
a shrill cry that tells us
in any language
the missing in action
are everywhere.

# Reflections on C Yard

Tuesday, early chow
the yard lieutenant calls herself
the Might Quinn
"one tough bitch," mirror glasses
reflect the lies
I feed her to keep myself fed.
But no lie
she looks like Edwina
my daughter who tells her friends
I died in a plane crash.

Last night I slept in the mouth
of a cave, swallowed
in the dripping night.
I wanted to keep Edwina safe,
but fear dug into my heart,
sandbagged useless feet
and she let go
and I knew I'd never find
a way out—I'd have to make
a life in that hole
like prehistoric fish on TV
gone blind, adjusting
to the lack of light.

In my bunk, staring up
at water stains, maps
for lost children, one of them
cries into a pee-stained quilt—
sobs, hollow and sharp
as night sticks on steel.
Brown eyes burn
through the darkness
but she can't deny

that day I worked the bees
from her clotted hair
or the stingers drilled
into my thumbs, puffed
to the size of burning cigars.

Tonight I roll a cigarette
on the yard, walk by
the Mexican TV—
a blonde woman points a gun at me,
I walk by the brother's TV
a baby climbs from a tire,
laughs at me.
It looks like someone spilled mercury
all over the yard
and the moon is stuck
on barb wire.
When I stand still and listen
I can hear big rigs on the freeway
smashing fireflies home
the breathing of children
only the blind can hear.

Big lights fill the sky
blank out the stars
like they never were—
but the tail of my eye
flashes with Edwina
rolling over in dreams
where she confesses all my crimes
where I have crept in
through the locked back door,
a cold draft of air,
a tune lodged with a buzzing
in her ear like bees
behind boarded windows and darkness
in a house left empty.

# Part 5 Sorrowful Mysteries

# Sorrowful Mysteries

A mystery is a sacred thing
that is difficult to understand.

Shoes
that hang in rearview mirrors
point to roads disappearing
behind, while time pulls
us forward over broken stars
and glass crusting the asphalt.
Corduroy slippers flatten in tar
and skid marks from a Caravan
loaded with children.
Where did you go
without so much as a shuffle
on the stairs?

A Tuesday in March, ghost gray
hazing the trees black
against a dingy sky. You skipped
rope past dinnertime, no one missed you
disappearing into higher and higher arcs
that touched the tip of heaven
your shoes skipped over the trees
left footprints where starlings hid
the list you dropped—tortillas, cocoa,
Ajax, salt—scraps of a red skirt
all they found in the shortcut alley.
How can we go on
without the music of your feet?

This time there were clues . . .
Hello Kitty pencil case, blue sailboat
barrettes, half-eaten Snowball,
sightings by barbers and stray
bird watchers . . . the crossing guard

who overheard your dream—
batting cobwebs and dust devils,
losing your shoes, every dark crevice
and stairwell that reached
for you, the tug at your skirt hem
wherever you ran, invisible shoes
tapping, but never found.
How can we bear the quiet now?

One shoe
departed from first steps
tottering in eight-millimeter snow
newly arrived on official oak,
marked state's evidence, its mate
lost among the jumble
of the fifty cent table
with broken rulers, stretch-marked belts
and chipped dice to roll
for one more deposition
seven come eleven
baby needs a new angel
one who won't sleep on the job
crack eggs on the wind—no priors
can outrun bullets, not afraid
to testify against us.

# 3:23 on Monday

A sudden burst of wind
herds the leaves
together in circles, whips
at shirttails, lapels,
and ropes of hair
flung into my eyes
the air, jumping blue
and electrical.
This is how
it must come, the end—
a sudden burst
like the train's blast
two minutes late
just passed through
the space I just passed
through, a hurtling
flash of blood and light
like entering or leaving
a lightning bolt,
crackling upward
to become the smallest blue
particle of sky.

Staggering, a blind man
crosses the station lot,
dodging the idling
and accelerating cars,
steps inside to count
his coins by touch
for a diet Coke.
Cool walls echo
the chime of nickels
and dimes, the songs
of Esso, Havoline
and Lysol that enter

two senses at once.
Stepping around him
like a slippery stone
I enter the blue heat
for one moment blinded
by a bolt of light swung
millions of years to hold me
numb in the eye
of its storm, smelling only
my own sweat
the last sense, they say
to go.

# Moulton Transformations*

*"If the universe has a heartbeat, its rate depends upon the hearer."* —Gary Zukov

*for Chuck Moulton, 1936–1995*


If it's Tuesday
on the corner of Olive and Wishon
and the sun has polarized its light
on Ophelia, Queen of the garbage bins
asleep behind the Golden Chinese Restaurant
her belly full of vanilla ice cream and chicken wings

and if the I Ching
of a shopping cart rattles
the alley behind the Brass Unicorn
where morning glories choke the flywheel
of a Plymouth Galaxy now in its fifth incarnation
as a museum of sycamore sun prints and musical belt
buckles

and if a black lab
who answers to Shadow
limps up from the Limbo world
of Old Saint Nick and kiss this
where some scientifically inexplicable
phenomenon has refracted the silver sphere

of the Tower Theater
through the cracked prism
of a Yamaha windshield, rainbowing
a river that floods from Olive and 99
all the way to the Sierra Nevadas and beyond
and if that yellow tiger kitty pees on a grimy fortune

that says "your TV set
will be trouble free for the next
ten years" . . . then maybe it's possible

to sing or breathe backwards, back to the moon
in a pool of spilled beer outside the Wild Blue
where Roy Bailey sweeps up the belly dancer's lost coins

and crushed joints
of the night before . . . and if
belief in solar explosions and
the fortuitous convergence of stars will do it
then perhaps the phone will ring once more and release
that old familiar, telepathic, horological, isochromatic,

irrevocable isosceles
growl that announces the spot
on the calendar marked by Shrodinger's cat
in a room moving beyond the boundaries of common sense
the Eternity of an hour on another ordinary First Tuesday
of course dependent on the relative velocity of the observer.

* Lorentz Transformations: equations that transform one
  observer's frame of reference into that of another's.

# April Elegy

*for Carl Zimmerman, d. April 22, 1994*

What we expected
were poppies puffing
out like applause—
polite rain fingering
the window slats,
a pinch of thyme, a snip
of dill and basil,
a lemon slice moon
to garnish the soufflé
of a tired season
rising into light.

What we got were nails
pared down to the moon
the repeated betrayal
of a train, arrived
too early or late,
blue jays riding
the cold hum of collect
calls at two A.M.
glass slapped, heaviness
of feathers fallen
out of flight.

# E Is in Heaven

*for Ernesto Trejo, 1950–1991*

E is in heaven
dancing with the moths
dreaming again
while fully awake,
a wide yard, faintly
familiar, a small
white worm asleep
in the heart of a rose.
The romantic anarchist
in perpetual love,
the overdrawn economist
maps a fortune
in tomorrow's dust,
the starry-eyed arsonist
sets beautiful fires
pauses for one last snapshot
in the garden
he only knows from the window
stoops over carrots,
soft hands posed on the hoe.

When rain falls
like memories of music
or breathing in sleep,
E is sitting still,
refusing to enter
or escape, refusing
to bow or applaud,
wanting to hold
what keeps slipping away,
the light, the sparrow,
speckled shadows flapping
from the sycamore

where he would perch
awhile longer
as the evening goes,
holding the last note
of a fading tune
we would refuse
to relinquish, if there were
any way on earth.

# Elegy for Jorge

*for my student, who took his own life*

Night nudges closer
dragging its broken wing
the great owl of midnight
throws its voice, a burden
for insomniacs
and newly hatched young

a pile of droppings
for the janitor
of sorrows who sweeps
the empty quad of torn
Scantrons and stars, all
the useless equations.

His drooping tune cannot
console us, nor
the sweep sweep of the wind.
Jorge, the owl begs
us to see how softly
we can rock you back

to call his bluff,
to nudge you from the narrow
landscape of your escape
a field frosted with straw
a cold nest to take
you back where you chipped

your hoe on morning's
backbone. If only
we could lure that quick
breathing from the thicket
where the nestling
curls around your soul.

But night is here, calling
to its brother,
the great owl of midnight
has thrown its voice—
even its heart
is full of broken wings.

# Elegy for the Artist

*"Go into yourself to find out if it's spreading out its roots in
the deepest places of your heart."—Rilke*

*for George Leroy, d. 1991*

Chicken feathers fly
at windshields
from the dirty, slatted truck
where live, boxed hens speed
to market in the fiery dust

of almond orchards
flowing past like rivers
heaped with flake white cargo
under a violet sky
smeared into hot gamboge.

Long haulers grind
down 99, gears growling
low and hungry into the wind.
Sides of beef rock through diesel
fog to the graveyard

shift at the meat plant
where the butcher whets his knife
on the edge of a morning star
as blue and solitary as steel.
He trims the gleam of fat

from a shank bone
and tosses the hoof to the moon—
all night pound, chop, pound
every strop on the steel
one tick closer to the hour

when he'll hook his apron,
bloodied like a Jackson Pollock,

behind the door
and step into new light
leaking from the skyline,

and for no earthly reason,
not commerce, not renown
not even a new set of uppers
to cure his crooked smile
he'll rush home

through chowdery fog
and with no bacon, eggs,
not even black coffee
to nourish him, he'll begin.
And with blood still on the moons

of his dark nails
the smell of it still in his hair
he'll rub out the second hand
for no reason other than the hunger
for color rooting in his heart.

# Summer Rain

*for Diane Trejo*

Eyes closed over despair
I can't even imagine, she listens
as I read, pause, then
skip over Lorca's Malagueña
Sabines' Black Butterflies,
fan the pages, asking
why there are no happy poems
except for childhood—
Machado's raindrops on windowpanes.
She likes Gloria Fuertes
leaning to see
what can be seen
from painted-on windows,
her face skips over pain
for a second . . . blurs
to a six-year-old's singsong light
that drips from the peaches
plunks the tomatoes
sweet with sun and dirt
whole days lost, drunk on sap
and cidery winds in the orchard.

Till a dark fluttering blots
the sun . . . and a voice
I can't hear calls her
back, pleads with her
to eat something, anything—
instead she sleeps all day
can't be left alone
all she once gave
to culling peaches and turning compost
now turned to the quiet battle within.

Stroking her shoulder,
it's soft and depthless

yet scaffolded with unseen bones
now housing the ground
where her own spores revolt
in a dark and fruitful mutiny.

Driving home, the road goes soft—
I can't see through the window
as if rain drops stroked it
lean forward to see
what can't be seen—
imagination
my oldest friend
is failing me—whispering
like an old man giving directions
to the mad. I turn away—
I don't want to see
down the next road—
I want to beg the earth
for one more summer rain
one more bumper crop of magic tomatoes,
but the wind whispers through the crack
of the window like pages turning
or black butterflies scattering home.

## Call 1-800-MARY

A man answers, says
we can leave a message
what do we expect
a miracle
or maybe some kind
of answer? Maybe
in the form of a question:
What is a quasar?
What is a cardinal sin?
Another name
for a baby swan?
Mother's neck, full of grace,
ready to strike cold eyes
on her winter nest
floating in the frozen
rushes, it must be
cold as sapphires there
in that icy womb
of stars where cells crack
apart like ice floes
holy roller of
dice, high mass of chemin
de fer, Virgo so far
away from home
no dime to call—
all the community
property in cold storage—
after ten years, we're told
it goes up for bid—
his gun still in the freezer
where she hid it
behind the top layer
of their wedding cake.
She has moved to Nome
with the two boys, left

him a ripped, down pillow
and restraining order.
He sells shoes at JCPenneys,
drinks Colt 45
at three A.M., calls out
for pork chow mein;
where is that order
of unconditional love
we were promised—
sinking under the frozen skin
of a lake, the hand brake
released? . . .
Someone's calling
in the night—
I'm calling you
Mother Mary—
a neon cross
and takeout Chinese bruise
through fog of a window;
the feverish moon touches my brow
these sheets growing colder.
I've done everything
I could think of, tucked
the quilt stitched with moon
and stars, even checked
for open pins.
In this night of gnawing,
must be squirrels
at the telephone wires,
someone's calling,
there's not much time,
these nervy wires grow thinner
something's going to give—
I'm calling you Mother
the fog thickens, water drips,
and the crib is filling inch
by inch.
I too am your child
Mother Mary.

# Acknowledgments

The following poems appeared in these publications:

"Amazing Grace," *Rattle* (1999).

"Nowhere Girl" as "The Chameleon," *The Black Warrior Review* (1994).

"Celeste Pareé," *The Journal* (Ohio State University, 1997).

"The Lost Underwear of Central Park," *Ploughshares* (1994).

"The Magic Hands Salon," *Quarterly West* (1996).

"Celebration Cake," *The Lowell Review* (1994).

"Taking It Back," *Unsettling America: An Anthology of Contemporary Multicultural Poetry,* edited by Maria M. Gillan and Jennifer Gillan (Penguin, 1994).

"American Meltdown," *Many Mountains Moving* (1996).

"Piñon Nuts," *Unsettling America: An Anthology of Contemporary Multicultural Poetry,* edited by Maria M. Gillan and Jennifer Gillan (Penguin, 1994); and *Glencoe Literature Library: Hispanic American Literature* (Glencoe/ McGraw Hill, 2000).

"I Always Check 'Other,' " *U.S. Latino Review* (2000).

"Rain at Night," *Hubbub* (1996).

"Why I'm Not Someone Else," *International Quarterly* (1994); and *Solo* (1997).

"Home Alone—Saturday Night," *The Lowell Review* (1994).

"Crazy Little Thing. . . ," *Montserrat Review* (1998).

"Meteor Showers, Yosemite," *The Geography of Home: California's Poetry of Place,* edited by Christopher Buckley and Gary Young (Heydey Books, 1999).

"Blong in America," *Night Sun* (1998).

"Cricket at CCWF," *Atlanta Review* (1995); *Solo* (1997); and *The Geography of Home: California's Poetry of Place,* edited by Christopher Buckley and Gary Young (Heydey Books, 1999).

"Moulton Transformations," *The Cimarron Review* (1996); and *The Geography of Home: California's Poetry of Place,* edited by Christopher Buckley and Gary Young (Heydey Books, 1999).

"E Is in Heaven," *The Geography of Home: California's Poetry of Place,* edited by Christopher Buckley and Gary Young (Heydey Books, 1999).

"Elegy for Jorge," *San Joaquin Review* (2000).

"Summer Rain," *How Much Earth: The Fresno Poets,* edited by Christopher Buckley, David Oliveira, and M. L. Williams (Heydey Books, 2001).

"Call 1-800-MARY," *Solo* (1997); and *Montserrat Review* (1998).

## About the Author

Dixie Salazar is a visual artist, poet, and novelist. Born in Chicago, Illinois, she grew up in the Midwest but has lived in California most of her life. She graduated from California State University, Fresno, with a Bachelor of Arts in both English and Art. In 1986 she received an MFA in Creative Writing from Columbia University in New York, where she also worked as Assistant Editor at *Parnassus: Poetry In Review.*

Salazar has worked as a courtroom artist, art therapist, teacher at a juvenile detention center, parenting teacher at the Fresno County Jail, and poetry teacher at Corcoran State Prison. She currently teaches creative writing at Valley State Prison for women and writing and literature at California State University, Fresno.

Her first book of poetry, *Hotel Fresno,* was published by Blue Moon Press in 1988, followed by *Reincarnation of the Commonplace,* which won the National Poetry Contest and was published by Salmon Run Press in 1998. *Limbo,* her first novel, was published by White Pine Press in 1995.